I Like the Fish

by P. J. Peregrine

Illustrated by Jetti Garrison

I Like the Fish
©2013 P. J. Peregrine

ISBN: 978-0-9833097-7-2
©2013 P. J. Peregrine

Published by:
Double Portion Publishing
1053 Eldridge Loop
Crossville, TN 38571
www.doubleportionpublishing.com

Illustrations by Jetti Garrison

Logo design of cats by Anna Elkins
www.annaelkins.com

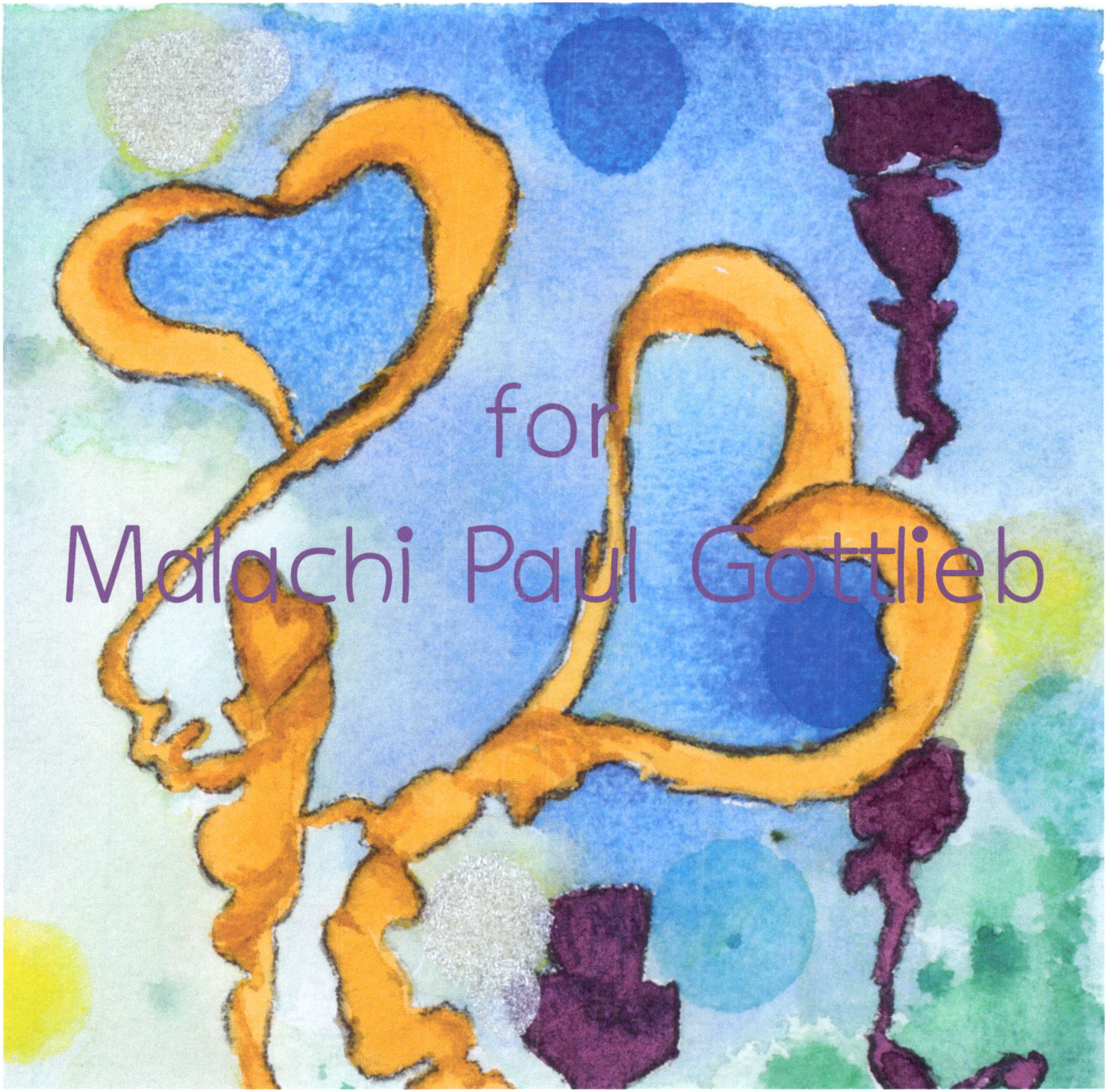
for
Malachi Paul Gottlieb

Hiding, still, or full of motion,

Fish are treasures in the ocean.

Fish that dart or duck or bubble.

Fish that live inside of rubble.

Fish that puff

and fish that kiss.

Fish that dive

and never miss.

Fish that look like butterflies.

Fish with bulging bubble-eyes.

Fish that sting

and fish that bite.

Peaceful fish

and fish that fight.

Fish like stars
and fish like jelly.

Fish that whistle from their belly.

Fish with squiggles,
fish with dots.
Fish with stripes and
frills and spots.

Fish with fancy tails that swish.

I love any kind of fish.

1. Royal Gamma Fish hide in caves in the ocean. Peek-a-boo!

2. Clownfish play hide and seek in their sea anemone homes.

3. Rock Mover Fish dig and move big rocks on the bottom of the ocean.

4. Kissing Gourami pucker their lips to give each other a big, fishy smooch.

5. Pufferfish can make themselves like a water balloon so no other fish can eat them.

6. Longnose Hawkfish wait for their food to come along, and then they dive and gobble it up.

7. Butterfly Fish use their pretty colors to hide in the corals.

8. Bubble Eye Goldfish have eyes like bubble gum bubbles.

9. Stingrays glide beneath the sea in groups called "fevers."

10. Piranhas have sharp teeth. Keep your hand out of their tank!

11. Rosy Barbs are peaceful. They don't fight with other fish.

12. Figi Blue Devil Damsel Fish like to pick a fight.

13. Starfish are sea animals shaped like a star, lounging around the ocean.

14. Jellyfish are sea animals that swim gracefully in all seas like little water ballerinas. But watch out! They can sting.

15. Toadfish boys make a whistling sound from their bellies to get the attention of toadfish girls. They are loud.

16. Lionfish wave their ruffles and show off their stripes.

17. Betta Fish have swishy tails like a silky fan.

www.ingramcontent.com/pod-product-compliance
Lightning Source LLC
Chambersburg PA
CBHW042057040426
42447CB00003B/261